Aquaponics for Beginners

How to Make an Aquaponic System and Raise Fish and Plants in the same Place. Produce Healthy Foods to Eat Healthy Foods.

© Copyright 2022 by **Philip L. Malave**

Philip L. Malave
Aquaponics for Beginners

© Copyright 2022 by Philip L. Malave - **All rights reserved**.

This Book is provided with the sole purpose of providing relevant information on a specific topic for which every reasonable effort has been made to ensure that it is both accurate and reasonable. Nevertheless, by purchasing this Book, you consent to the fact that the author, as well as the publisher, are in no way experts on the topics contained herein, regardless of any claims as such that may be made within. As such, any suggestions or recommendations that are made within are done so purely for entertainment value. It is recommended that you always consult a professional prior to undertaking any of the advice or techniques discussed within.

This is a legally binding declaration that is considered both valid and fair by both the Committee of Publishers Association and the American Bar Association and should be considered as legally binding within the United States.

The reproduction, transmission, and duplication of any of the content found herein, including any specific or extended information, will be done as an illegal act regardless of the end form the information ultimately takes. This includes copied versions of the work, both physical, digital, and audio, unless express consent of the Publisher is provided beforehand. Any additional rights reserved.

Furthermore, the information that can be found within the pages described forthwith shall be considered both accurate and truthful when it comes to the recounting of facts. As such, any use, correct or incorrect, of the provided information will render the Publisher free of responsibility as to the actions taken outside of their direct purview. Regardless, there are zero scenarios where the original author or the Publisher can be deemed liable in any fashion for any damages or hardships that may result from any of the information discussed herein.

Additionally, the information in the following pages is intended only for informational purposes and should thus be thought of as universal. As befitting its nature, it is presented without assurance regarding its prolonged validity or interim quality. Trademarks that are mentioned are done without written consent and can in no way be considered an endorsement from the trademark holder.

Philip L. Malave
Aquaponics for Beginners

CONTENTS

INTRODUCTION 5

CHAPTER 1 - Aquaponics 7

   Brief Historical Note 7

   What is Aquaponics? 10

   How does Aquaponics work? 12

   Main applications of Aquaponics 18

CHAPTER 2 - Advantages and Disadvantages 29

   Advantages of Aquaponic Growing 29

   Disadvantages of Aquaponic Growing 31

CHAPTER 3 - Types of Aquaponic System 35

   Choice of location 36

   Exposure to light 37

   Location 40

   Shading Structures 41

   Fish tanks 43

CHAPTER 4 - Media Beds, NFT, DWC 61

   Water movement 62

   Submersible water pump 63

   Airlifts 65

   Muscular strength 66

   Ventilation 66

Water flow dynamics..69

Construction of a Growbed 71

CHAPTER 5 - Aquaponics how to make a plant 75

What does it take to start? 77

How to start? 81

CHAPTER 6 - How to Make an Aquaponic System at Home 85

Prepare the Frame...85

Hydraulic System 86

CHAPTER 7 - Which plants? 95

CHAPTER 8 - Which Fishes in Aquaponics? 99

Carp koi, gambusie and medaka 100

Gobion, sturgeon and shellfish 102

Fish in Aquaponics for food purposes 103

CONCLUSION... 111

INTRODUCTION

Aquaponics is a way of growing plants in water while also using fish farming to give all of the necessary mineral nutrients. The good news is that the entire cultivation process is highly automated, but it still necessitates meticulous supervision.

Aquaponics is preferred because it makes use of aquaculture water and nutrients, which are given straight to the plant's roots.

Lighting is also a significant factor in agricultural production. Planting crops in vertical buildings maximizes access to light while keeping density and shade to a minimum, resulting in enough lighting.

In terms of water, nutrients, and light, these growing conditions for plant cultivation are perfect for crops, maximizing the value of the growing area and utilizing space that would otherwise be useless. Using a moveable multi-level cultivation structure ensures that plants are exposed to optimal illumination throughout the growth season.

Philip L. Malave
Aquaponics for Beginners

CHAPTER 1 - Aquaponics

Due to climate change and the international economic crisis, there is a clear need for the agri-food sector to identify new strategies to ensure more sustainable production in line with new market needs. Farmers and agricultural producers are in fact called upon to face the challenges arising from climate change and its effects on the environment, biodiversity and the living conditions of the population. The water scarcity that has affected various regions of the world in recent years has put farmers and fish farmers under severe strain, with their production reduced or greatly damaged. In this context, aquaponics could represent a real possibility for the development of this sector. But what is aquaponics and how does it work?

Brief Historical Note

In the Western world, a strong impulse has been generated in the last decade to study integrated systems of breeding and cultivation that exploit the natural synergistic relationships existing between plants and animals to obtain production of aquatic and terrestrial plant species, with minimum human environmental impact and respecting the conservation of water and energy resources.

Thanks to the research started more than thirty years ago first in the United States and later in Australia, it has now become possible to produce freshwater crayfish in one's own backyard or raise edible or ornamental fish while growing, for example, tomatoes, zucchini, basil and salad directly inside covered structures in the city centre, without needing either land or a substantial water source.

This "miracle" has been made possible thanks to the development of effective water recirculation and recovery systems that work in perfect synergy with vegetable biofiltration equipment in a completely natural regime.

The eco-sustainable recirculation systems used in this way can be sized to meet both the food and economic needs of a single family and the wider expectations of commercial production, aimed at supplying edible aquatic and vegetable species to local markets, supermarkets, restaurants and food distribution chains, guaranteeing them a constant supply of high organoleptic quality throughout the year.

Commercial plants of this kind (called aquaponic systems) have arisen in recent years in several countries such as the United States, Canada, Mexico, Germany and Great Britain, while other countries such as China and Thailand, already large operators in the Aquaculture sector, have become interested in this more eco-sustainable and efficient production method for the production of fish, shrimp and edible vegetables.

In Japan in particular, aquaponic systems have been installed in the basements of some skyscrapers or in premises adjacent to organic restaurants and contribute with their operation to provide fresh food at zero kilometres to the local inhabitants.

In the United States, real urban aquaponic farms have been created that have allowed the recovery of warehouses and other disused buildings, reconverting them in an ecological way and making them the productive heart of farmer markets that can offer not only vegetable products but also freshwater fish products such as trout, catfish, carp, tilapia.

In 2012 the largest aquaponics plant was inaugurated in the Arab Emirates; the Emirates import about 85% of their food because of their difficulty in cultivating in their territory. This dependence means that market fluctuations and supply problems have a greater impact on them in terms of food deficit.

The Baniyas Center (this is the name of the aquaponic plant) can produce as many as 200 tons of fish and 300 thousand heads of lettuce every year, helping to reduce the use of imports and providing greater food security for the nation. In addition, thanks to the way the system recycles water, the water is expected to remain usable for a year or more inside the tanks without the need to replace it.

What is Aquaponics?

If we want to cut short we could give an answer like this: "Aquaponics is the marriage between aquaculture (fish farming) and hydroponic plant growth in water, in the absence of soil)" Put together in an integrated system and, since we have integrated the system, why not also integrate the name? Aquaponics then.

Therefore, aquaponics can be defined as the union between aquaculture and hydroponics. The latter is a practice in which plants are grown without soil, using only water enriched with all the nutrients that plants need. In the case of aquaponics, the basic nutrients for plant growth are provided by fish farming, of which these substances are the main waste products. In this system, elements such as nitrogen and phosphorus, resulting both from excretion and excretion of fish and from decomposition of uningested feed, can be absorbed by the roots of growing plants directly immersed in the water.

Aquaponics is not a new cultivation technique; in fact, it is since the 70s that we have started to talk about this technique in a substantial way. However, it is only in recent years that it has returned to the forefront, thanks also to new scientific research and greater attention to sustainability on the part of consumers and producers.

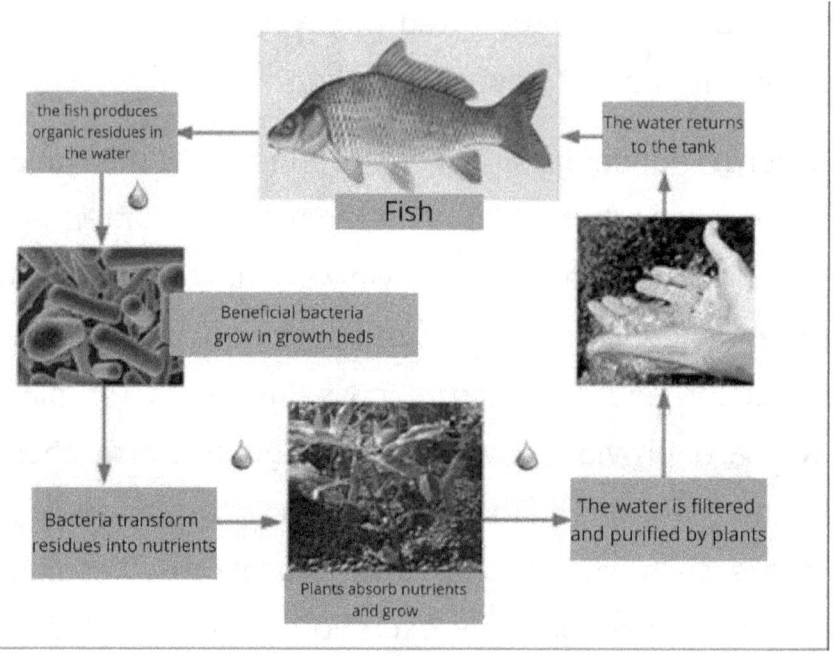

How does Aquaponics work?

An aquaponic system is a recirculation system, where the water, thanks to the use of one or more pumps, is taken from the tank in which the fish are bred and passed through a biofilter. The latter allows to start the nitrification process that will lead to the formation of nitrites and nitrates then assimilated by the plants. In addition, it will reduce as much as possible the quantity of suspended solids, which is very important in order to maintain the good quality of the water and avoid the lowering of the dissolved oxygen in it. The water is then introduced into the cultivation beds in which the cultivated plants are present (whose roots are in direct contact with the water) and finally reintroduced into the breeding tank.

There are many varieties of cultivated plants, not only leafy vegetables but also plants such as zucchini, aubergines, tomatoes or aromatic herbs. Likewise, it is possible to breed almost all freshwater fish species in aquaponics, from trout to carp (but also ornamental species such as Koi carp) or even species that are exotic to us such as tilapia. It is also possible to breed various species of crustaceans such as the Austropotamobius pallipes crayfish in aquaponics. Depending on the animal and plant species chosen, the system should be calibrated to ensure the correct supply of nutrients to the plants.

Aquaponics can be understood as a sustainable agricultural production activity in which the cycles of the main macronutrients are closed through the integration of two production systems, aquaculture and hydroponics. Compared to conventional farming techniques, aquaponics has several strengths, including:

Water saving aquaponics uses about 90% less water than traditional agriculture.

Small spaces: As plants do not need soil, aquaponics allows intensive cultivation in relatively small spaces.

No use of pesticides and pesticides: aquaponics does not include their use. In order to avoid problems of toxicity to fish and plants, biological control is used in aquaponics to control parasites. In addition, an attempt is made to isolate the production system as well as possible from the surrounding environment in order to limit the entry of pests and pathogens.

No fertiliser use: plant nutrients are provided by fish farming

Emissions control: there is no need to use agricultural vehicles, resulting in lower consumption of fossil fuels.

What are the limits of aquaponics?

The main limits of aquaponics concern two fundamental aspects: the complexity of the production system and its economic sustainability. Being an integrated production system, aquaponics requires expertise from the farmer/breeder both in the cultivation of plant species and in fish farming.

From an economic point of view, aquaponics can generate a double profit for those who practice it by placing two different types of products (vegetables and fish) on the market. On the other hand, the need to allocate these systems inside greenhouses or protected structures and to condition the temperature in order to guarantee a constant production during the year, increase production costs. But now this is the price that consumers must get used to paying for a truly sustainable product.

Which plants can be grown with aquaponics?

There are many varieties of plants that can be grown with the aquaponics method, potentially all of them; in particular all those - as seen above - that do not need any special support to grow, including broad-leaved vegetables, salads, zucchini, aubergines and aromatic herbs.

Which fish for aquaponics?

For fish that can be used within an aquaculture system, you can choose any type of freshwater fish, including shrimps. Of course, depending on the type of fish chosen, it is necessary to set the system differently, according to the characteristics of the variety chosen, in order to ensure the right amount and type of nutrients to the plants.

What does it take to create an aquaculture plant?

To build an aquaculture plant from scratch you need to buy a tank for fish farming, a hydroponic tank with a pump - which will be placed above the fish tank - in which you will place the plants, bacteria that allow you to decompose the waste fish, filters, a kit to measure and adjust the pH, supplements to solve any problems and nutritional deficiencies and then of course the fish you prefer and the plants to be grown.

To start and start with peace of mind an aquaculture, it is advisable to buy a system and ready-to-use kits, which will only need to be assembled and set up following the instructions in the package. Generally speaking, starting and maintenance of an aquaponic system does not require great care and attention, but - like all crops of this type, including hydroponics and aeroponics - it requires some controls, such as proper temperature, pH, humidity, proper ventilation and aeration, cleaning of surfaces and the right amount of nutrients.

One of the important aspects to consider at the beginning, in fact, is precisely the relationship - which must be well balanced - between the number and type of plants chosen and the number and breed of fish you wish to breed. In this way you can ensure a healthy and efficient environment. The other factor to keep in mind always is the nutrition provided to the fish, which must be of high quality and supplied in the right doses in order to guarantee the balance of the environment.

Main applications of Aquaponics

The technique of soil cultivation in aquaponic ecosystem allows to grow 100% organic plants with different application methods depending on the desired crops.

Vertical Aquaponics Vertical Growing

Vertical cultivation increases the convenience of the plant cost on the available space, optimizing the human labour cost. Vertical cultivation can be used to seasonally or deseasonally adjust plant production (light conditions and controlled environment).

How much does vertical aquaponic cultivation produce?
- Lettuce: 95 kg/m2 each year
- Chard: 75 kg/m2 each year
- Strawberries: 4.9Kg/m2 each month (Seascape)

- Basil: 1.88 kg/m2 per week Vs 0.15 kg/m2 of ground cultivation!

ZipGrow is a patented vertical hydroponic technology designed for high density agricultural production. The growth towers ensure the maximization of crop production, which is up to 4 times more intense than traditional techniques. The vertical towers consist of a rigid casing that contains the multifunctional Matrix Media. It is a growing substrate as well as a mechanical and biological filter.

The matrix inside each tower is an essential component of the system, their surface area is much larger than any other inert, this allows a greater nitrifying and filtering power, which is the basis of high-density production. The length of these matrices is 1,50 mt making it very easy to install and maintain, moreover it is composed by 93% air, allowing the water to move freely inside.

The thrust of the water dissolves oxygen inside it, thus eliminating the formation of anaerobic zones, which are harmful for an aquaponic cultivation plant because they tend to cause plant roots to die, cause foul-smelling compounds such as hydrogen sulphite and are home to some pathogenic organisms. Open spaces and good percolation, on the contrary, allow a more stable temperature in the roots, which is the basis of plant health.

Why choose vertical cultivation?

Current agricultural practices are unsustainable:

- Water is treated as an infinite resource.
- Our agricultural efforts absorb resources such as water and land and make obvious use of pesticides.
- Between 38 and 50% of harvested produce is lost to deterioration.

Nutrient Film Technique

The Nutrient Film Technique is a cultivation technique that uses horizontal PVC pipes, in each of which passes a film of water rich in nutrients. One of the advantages of using this technique is its low evaporation, as the water is completely shielded from the sun.

Holes are drilled in the pipe, in which the plants will be placed. As soon as they receive the nutrient flow, they start to develop the root system inside the pipe, at the same time the stems and leaves start to grow all around.

The NFT does not use inerts, so the water passing through the pipes must necessarily be treated beforehand, so a mechanical separator and a biofilter are required.

The maximum flow rate, within each pipe, must always be controlled and should never exceed 1-2 litres/minute.

In this project will be used no. 6 φ110 ducts, each of which will have a length of 5.00 m and a slope of about 1 cm/m. The holes inside each pipe have a diameter of about 8 cm and a wheelbase of 50 cm. The distance between two pipes will be 1.0 m to allow the passage of one person.

The NFT channels/pipes will be raised from the ground with adjustable structures, in order to create a natural waterfall for the collection of wastewaters and the natural recirculation to the collection tank, equipped with a submersible pump.

Growth Bed

Growth beds are a technique used for high-medium-stem crops or for plants that produce large and/or heavy fruits. The aggregates used inside these beds in fact act both as support for the roots of the plants and as filtration, in theory, mechanics and biology.

The mechanical filtration of these aggregates may be lacking in cases where the density of fish is very high. For this reason and for safety reasons, it was preferred to use a mechanical separator located inside the fish tanks.

The weak points of this technique are essentially two: the high evaporation of the water and the weight of the aggregates. However, if you want to cultivate certain types of plants there is no alternative: even in the trunk tree area the technique used is precisely that of the growth beds (in structure more similar to pots than "beds" proper), as the mechanical resistance of the Aquaponic is the only one among the cultivation techniques capable of bearing the weight of a trunk tree.

The structure of the growth beds (in the dedicated thematic area) will be made of laminated wood, covered with food-grade polyethylene, to guarantee the hydraulic seal. There is a total of 4 growth beds, all measuring 0.70 mt x 4.50 mt x 0.30 mt; the inert material chosen is expanded clay, given its chemical-physical characteristics. The density of cultivation that can be reached with this method strongly depends on the type of plant used: it varies from a value of 6 plants/m2 in the case of watermelons, up to values of about 200 plants/m2 in the case of saffron.

Fundamental in order to guarantee the movement of water within the system is the siphon.

The siphon allows the water to rise to a specific level, allowing the roots of the plants to take all the nutrients present in it and, once the maximum height has been reached, triggering it allows the tank to be emptied by sending the water to the return tank.

Deep water culture

Functioning:

The nutrient-rich water is circulated through long channels at a depth of about 20 cm while the rafts (usually polystyrene) float on top. The plants are supported inside holes in the rafts. The roots of the plants hang in nutrient-rich, oxygenated water, where they absorb large amounts of oxygen and nutrients that contribute to fast growing conditions.

This method is the most common in large scale distribution, when you tend to grow a specific crop (typically lettuce, salad leaves or basil) and where you have a high density of fish (up to 10-20 kg of fish per m3 of aquarium). However, it can be adapted to a low-density coefficient of fish production.

The water flows by gravity from the fish tanks, through the mechanical filter and into the biofilter. The water is pumped in two directions through a "Y" connector. Some water is pumped directly into the fish tank, the remaining water is distributed equally through the channels. The water flows, again by gravity, through the growth channels where the plants are located and then out of the channels and back into the biofilter, where it is pumped back into the tank or fish channels.

However, when using a low fish density, the DWC can be designed without the use of external, mechanical or biological filtration containers. In this system, water flows by gravity from the fish tanks directly into the DWC channels.

Advantages:

The main advantage of the DWC is the amortisation of all initial costs.

It is a good alternative for beginner growers interested in growing above ground. In addition, let us not forget that the most important results will be achieved at harvest time. Higher nutrient uptake also means plants with higher quality buds, higher yields and a more intense "high". Soil cultivation will never be able to compete with hydroponic cultivation, as the roots do not receive the same amount of oxygen provided by a constant flow of air. Moreover, it is a system that can be expanded. The principle is also the same for growing several plants.

CHAPTER 2 - Advantages and Disadvantages

Advantages of Aquaponic Growing

The advantages of aquaponics are many, let's analyse them together:

Few resources

One of the most considered is its ability to grow different types of food using very few resources in the process. In fact, it is a natural and organic process.

Minimum use of electricity

To operate an aquaponic cultivation system you need power, but there are few pieces of equipment that require energy. This leads to low net energy consumption.

Minimum water use

Even less water is used because most aquaponics systems are recirculated, which means that the water is circulated through the system instead of being disposed of after use.

The loss of primary water in aquaponic systems is minimal because it comes from evaporation and transpiration of the plants.

No use of pesticides and chemicals

Equally important is that in many systems the need for pesticides and other chemicals is low and sometimes not needed at all.

Aquaponics systems are designed for use in a controlled environment, such as a greenhouse or indoor warehouse, and the process by which bacteria convert fish waste into plant food or nutrients eliminates the need for fertilizers.

The pH is also adjusted by itself within the system through the process of conversion by the bacteria.

Disadvantages of Aquaponic Growing

Of course, it's not all pink and flowers, there are also disadvantages in aquaponic cultivation. Let's go together and see what they are.

Non-economic start-up cost

The start-up cost is often higher than what people want to spend on the cultivation system.

While you may think that these systems are cheap, you will notice that systems at the practitioner's level tend to be quite expensive. However, this expense begins to pay for itself as you start enjoying fresh produce after a short time.

Difficulties in choosing the system best suited to our needs

The choices between the available systems can be quite difficult to make. While you may think that there is only one system style, you will quickly find more systems available.

A simple choice in the wrong system, however, can lead to a disaster because the system will not be suitable for the use you want to make of it.

Daily Maintenance

Daily checks must be carried out on systems, lights and pipes. These checks will help to ensure that the system is working properly but will also help to ensure that everything is working properly. Without this type of control, people may have trouble understanding why their plants are not thriving.

Is it good to grow in aquaponics?

Aquaponic systems are an easy way to grow food.

Daily maintenance is necessary, but once the system is in operation, the main activity, day by day, is to feed the fish and check for signs of change in the balance of the system. Monitoring water chemistry, temperature and nutrient levels and moving to correct them as needed will maintain a thriving aquaponic system.

I recommend starting with the type of cultivation that meets your needs and expectations.

Philip L. Malave
Aquaponics for Beginners

CHAPTER 3 - Types of Aquaponic System

This chapter illustrates drawings related to the design of different aquaponics systems. There are many design aspects to consider, to consider all environmental and biological factors that have an impact on the aquaponic ecosystem. The purpose of this chapter is to present all these aspects in the most accessible way in order to provide a comprehensive explanation of each component of an aquaponic system.

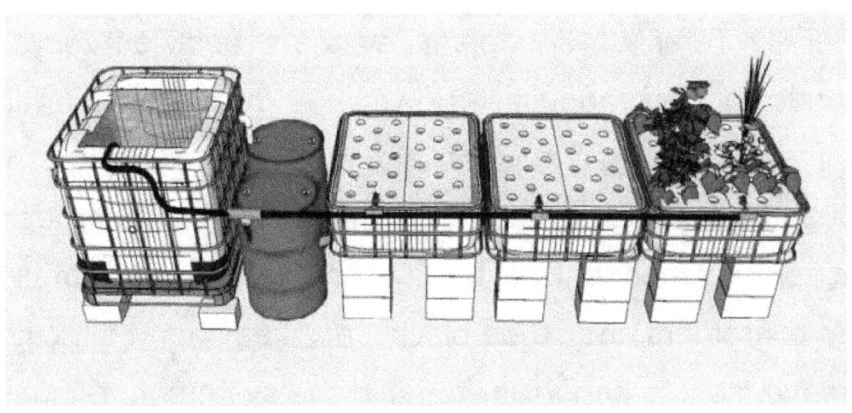

Floating Root Planting Drawing (DWC)

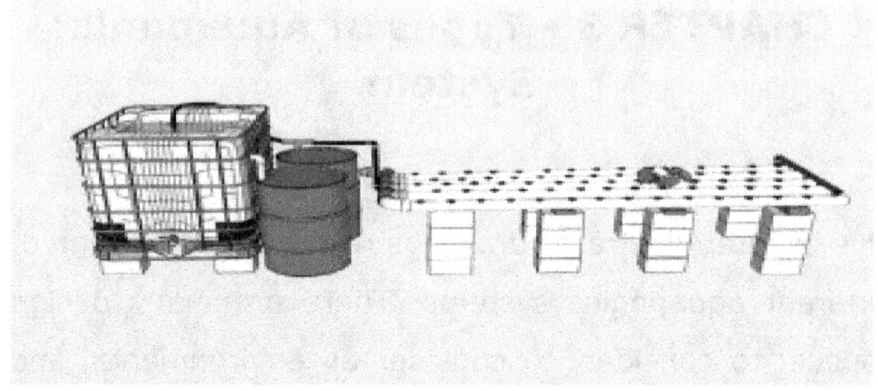

Drawing a small plant (NFT)

Choice of location

The choice of site is an important aspect in the installation of an aquaponic system. In this section we generally refer to aquaponic systems built outdoors, without a greenhouse. However, there are brief comments on greenhouses and shading using mesh structures for larger units. It is important to remember that some components of the system, particularly water-filled containers and stone blocks, are heavy and difficult to move, so it is important to build the system in its final position. The locations identified must be on a stable, horizontal surface, in an area that is protected from bad weather but well exposed to sunlight.

Make sure you choose a site that is stable and level. Some of the main components of an aquaponic system are heavy, there is a real risk that the legs of the system will sink into the ground. This can lead to the interruption of water flow, flooding or a catastrophic collapse of the system. It is therefore essential to find a flat, solid ground. Implanting everything on a concrete surface can be a solution, but it has the disadvantage of not being able to pass any of the components underground, therefore with the risk of tripping. If the system is placed on the ground, it is useful to cover everything with sheets that prevent the growth of weeds. In addition, it may be essential to place concrete or cement blocks under the legs of the grow beds to improve their stability.

Exposure to light

Extreme environmental conditions can stress plants and destroy structures. Strong winds can have a considerable negative impact on plant production and can cause damage to stem and reproductive parts.

In addition, heavy rain can damage plants and unprotected electrical outlets. Large amounts of rain can dilute nutrient-rich water and can flood the system if there is no overflow mechanism. Snow causes the same problems as heavy rainfall, with the added threat of cold damage. It is advisable that the system is in a protected wind zone. If heavy rainfall is usual, it may be worth protecting the system with a plastic cover (tunnel or greenhouse).

Sunlight is crucial for plants, which need to receive the optimal amount of sunlight during the day. Most common aquaponic systems grow well in full sunlight; however, if the sunlight is too intense, a simple structure that allows shading can be installed above the growing beds. Some photosensitive plants, including lettuce, and some cabbages may rise to seed due to too much sun or become bitter or take a bad taste. Other tropical plants, such as turmeric and some ornamental plants may show burns on the leaves when exposed to too much sun and therefore produce better if they can be placed in half shade. On the opposite side, with little sunlight, some plants can have slow growth rates. Therefore, we should be careful to build the aquaponic plants in a sunny position. If a shaded area is the only one available, it is recommended that suitable species are planted.

The systems should be designed to take advantage of the moving sun in the sky from east to west. Generally, growth beds should be spatially arranged so that the longest side is on the north-south axis. This is more efficient than the sun during the day. Alternatively, if it is preferable to have less light, depending on the type of crop, orient the beds, tubes and channels following the east-west axis. Also pay attention to the layout of the plants, which should not inadvertently become one with the other.

Unlike plants, fish do not need direct sunlight. On the contrary, it is important that the fish tanks are in the shade, which is why they are usually covered with shading sheets.

Shading helps to keep the water temperature stable and prevent algae from growing, covering fish tanks also prevents debris or leaves from falling into them and prevents intrusion by ichthyophagous animals.

Location

When choosing the site, it is important to consider the availability of connections to the services. Electrical sockets are required for water and air pumps that must be protected from water and equipped with a "lifesaving" device to reduce the risk of electric shock.

In addition, the water supply to the system should be easily accessible, whether it is for connections to the municipal network or rainwater collection tanks.

Although extremely efficient in terms of water resources, aquaponic systems require water additions from time to time, filters should also be rinsed. If an aquaponic system were located near a 'traditional' crop, it would benefit from rinsing the filters, which are always rich in nutrients. The system should also be placed where it is easy to access every day because frequent monitoring and daily feeding of the fish is necessary. Finally, consider fencing the entire system to prevent theft and vandalism, the entry of predatory animals and for compliance with any food safety rules.

Shading Structures

Having a greenhouse is not essential for a small aquaponic system but having a roof can be useful because it lengthens the production season. This is particularly true in colder temperate regions, greenhouses can also be used to maintain a warm water temperature during the cold months, allowing year-round production.

A greenhouse is a metal, wood or plastic frame that is covered with transparent nylon, plastic or glass. The purpose of this structure is to allow sunlight (solar radiation) to enter the greenhouse and remain "trapped" in it, thus heating the air inside the greenhouse. When the sun goes down, the heat is retained in the greenhouse by the roof and walls, allowing a warmer and more stable temperature throughout the 24 hours. Greenhouses also provide environmental protection against wind, snow and driving rain. In greenhouses, the growing season can be extended by maintaining solar heat, but they can also be heated from the inside. Greenhouses can also keep animals and other pests away. Greenhouses are comfortable for working during the cold season and offer the farmer protection from the weather. All in all, these advantages can be summed up in increased productivity and a longer farming season.

However, these advantages must be offset by the negative aspects of greenhouses. The initial investment costs for a greenhouse can be high depending on the desired degree of technology and sophistication. Greenhouses also require additional operating costs because fans are needed to create air circulation to prevent overheating and excessive humidity conditions.

Fish tanks

Fish tanks are a key component in any plant and can account for up to 20 percent of the total cost. Fish require certain conditions to live and thrive and therefore fish tanks must be chosen carefully. There are several important aspects to consider such as shape, material and colour.

The shape of the tank

Although any shape would be fine, round tubs with flat bottoms are the best. The round shape allows the water to circulate evenly and at the same time the solid waste is conveyed to the centre of the tank by centripetal force. Flat-bottomed square tanks are also acceptable, but they require more work in solid waste removal. Other tanks, artistic and non-geometric in shape, with many curves can create dead spots where there is water without circulation. These areas can collect waste and create dangerous anoxic conditions for fish. If you must use irregularly shaped tanks it may be necessary to add water or air pumps to ensure proper circulation and remove solids. It is also important to choose a tank that adapts to the characteristics of the aquatic species kept some species have better growth and less stress with adequate space available.

Material

The use of inert plastic or fibreglass is recommended for their long life. Avoid metal due to rust. Plastic and fibreglass tanks are interesting to install (also for hydraulic connections) and are quite light and easy to handle. They are commonly used, even old containers (plastic tanks for transporting liquids and blue bins) as they tend to be cheap. If you use such containers make sure they are UV resistant because direct sunlight can destroy plastic. Generally, low density polyethylene (LDPE) tanks are preferable because of their high resistance and the characteristics that allow them to be used for food. LDPE in fact, is the most used material for water tanks for civil use. Another option is an earth pond. Natural ponds are very difficult to manage for aquaponic plants because the natural biological process that occurs inside the substrate and in the mud at the bottom can be difficult to govern and its nutrients are often already used by aquatic plants. Cement or plastic lined ponds are much more acceptable and can be an economical option.

Soil ponds can make hydraulic operations difficult and plumbing design should be carefully considered before embracing this option. One of the simplest ponds is a hole dug into the ground, lined with bricks or concrete blocks, and then lined

with a waterproof coating like polyethylene plastic. Other options include second-hand containers such as bathtubs, drums or bulk containers. It is very important to ensure that the container has not previously been used for toxic materials to prevent any trace of it remaining. So, choose a used container carefully, best if you know the seller.

The colour white or other light colours are strongly recommended as they allow easy control of the fish to check its behaviour and the amount of waste deposited on the bottom of the tank. White tanks also reflect sunlight and keep the water cooler. Alternatively, the outside of dark coloured tanks can be painted white. In very hot or cold areas, it may be necessary to further insulate the tanks thermally.

Fish tanks should be covered. The shade prevents algae from growing. In addition, the cover serves to prevent the fish from jumping out (this often occurs with freshly inserted fish or if the water quality is not optimal), the cover also serves to prevent leaves and debris from falling into the tanks and to prevent predators such as cats and birds from attacking the fish. Shading nets are often used for agriculture that block up to 80-90 percent of the sunlight. Shading nets can be secured to a simple wooden frame to provide weight, prevent the wind from moving them and at the same time allow easy removal.

Safety and redundancy

The first precaution to be taken with respect to fish tanks is to prevent them from losing water, with the danger of losing all the fish. Even if some accidents are inevitable (for example a tree falling on the tank), mistakes with more serious effects are almost always due to the "human factor". Therefore, make sure that there is no possibility for the operator to discharge the water inadvertently. If the water pump is in the fish tank, never place it on the bottom so that the tank cannot be brought to dry. Always use a hose inside the tank to ensure a minimum water level.

Filtering

Mechanical filtering

For a recirculation system, mechanical filtration is undoubtedly the most important aspect of the project. From a mechanical point of view, filtration is the separation and removal of suspended solids and fish waste from tanks. Removing this waste is essential for the health of the system, because otherwise, if solid waste is broken down into fish tanks, harmful gases released by anaerobic bacteria would be released. In addition, the waste can clog the systems and disrupt the water flow, causing anoxic conditions that are hostile to root development.

Small-scale aquaponic systems generally have a lower stocking density than the traditional recirculation fish farming systems for which these mechanical filters were originally designed, but a certain level of mechanical filtration is also essential for aquaponic fish tanks, regardless of the type of hydroponic method used.

There are different types of mechanical filters. The simplest method is a screen or filter between the fish tank and the growth beds. This filter catches solid waste and must be rinsed frequently.

Similarly, the water leaving the fish tank can pass through a small container of particulate matter, separated from the growth bed; this container is easier to rinse periodically.

Both these methods are valid for some small-scale aquaponic systems, but are insufficient in larger systems with more fish, where the amount of solid waste is significant.

There are many types of mechanical filters, sedimentation tanks, radial flow filters, sand or bead filters, etc. each can be used depending on the amount of solid waste that needs to be removed. However, since this publication focuses on small-scale aquaponic systems, sedimentation tanks and mechanical separators are the most appropriate filters.

Sedimentation tanks, in general, can remove up to 60 percent of total solids. For more information on the different mechanical filtration methods, see the additional reading section at the end of this publication.

Mechanical Separators

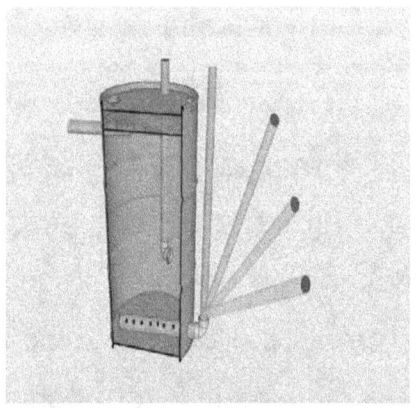

A mechanical separator is a dedicated vessel that uses the properties of water to separate particles. Generally, water that moves slower is not capable of carrying as many particles as fast flowing water. Therefore, the separator is constructed to accelerate and slow down the water so that the particles concentrate at the bottom and can be removed. In a separator turbulence is created, water from the fish tank enters close to the centre of gravity through a pipe. This pipe is positioned tangentially to the container and forces the water to swirl in a circular motion inside the container. The centripetal force created by the circular movement of the water forces the solid waste into the water at the centre and bottom of the container, because the water in the centre of the vortex is slower than the water outside. Once this happens the waste is collected at the bottom. A hose attached to the bottom of the container can be opened periodically, allowing solid waste to be removed from the container and used for traditional watering. The cleaned water comes out of the top separator and enters the biofilter or growth beds.

The trapped and removed solid waste contains nutrients and is very useful for traditional crops or garden plants in general. As a general guideline, for small-scale plants the size of the mechanical separator should be about one sixth of the volume of the fish tank but many factors such as the storage density of the fish and the design of the tank and the separator itself influence the size. Appendix 8 will contain detailed, step-by-step instructions for the construction of each part of these systems.

Proper preliminary mechanical filtration is particularly important for NFT and DWC units and serves to intercept and remove solid waste. Without this preliminary process, the solid waste in suspension would accumulate in vegetable growth pipes and canals and suffocate the roots. The accumulation of solid waste causes blockages in the pumps and hydraulic components. Finally, as mentioned, unfiltered waste can create anaerobic points in the circuit that threaten the system. These anaerobic zones can in fact lead to the development of bacteria that produce hydrogen sulphide, a toxic and lethal gas for fish, due to the fermentation of solid waste. The presence of dangerous anaerobic zones is often revealed by the smell of rotten eggs.

Biofiltration

Biofiltration is the conversion of ammonia and nitrite into nitrates by living bacteria. Most fish waste is not filterable using a mechanical filter because the waste is dissolved directly in the water and the size of these particles is too small to be removed mechanically. Therefore, an aquaponic system uses microscopic bacteria to treat this microscopic waste. Biofiltration is essential because in aquaponics ammonia and nitrite are toxic even at low concentrations, while plants need nitrates to grow. In an aquaponic system, the biofilter is deliberately designed to accommodate as many living bacteria as possible. In addition, the movement of water within a biofilter will be useful to break down very fine solids not extracted from the separator.

Separate biofiltration is not necessary in a medium bed cultivation technique (e.g. expanded clay) because the grow beds themselves are perfect biofilters.

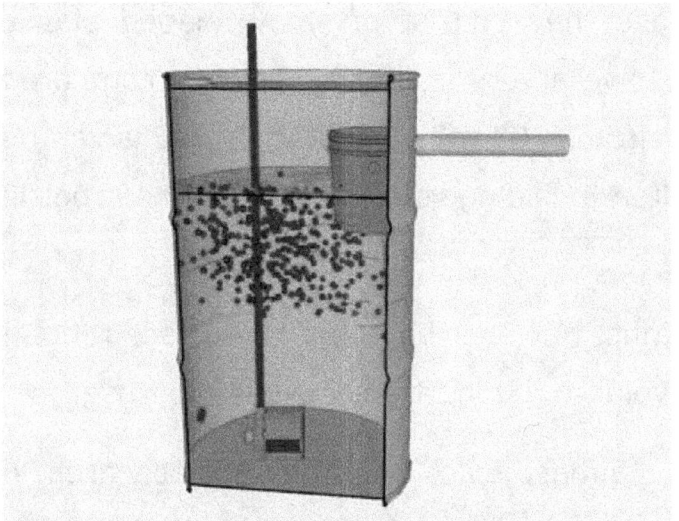

The biofilter is designed to have a large surface area fed with well oxygenated water. The biofilter is installed between the mechanical filter and the containers in which the hydroponic culture takes place. The minimum volume of the biofilter should be one sixth of that of the fish tank.

The "mediom" commonly used in the biofilter is Bioballs® a registered product available in aquaculture shops, there are also generic brands.

These products are designed to be an ideal biofilter material because they consist of small shaped plastic elements that have a very large surface area compared to their volume (500-700 m2 / m³). Other media can be used as a biofilter, including volcanic gravel, plastic bottle caps, etc.

Each biofilter must however have a high surface ratio in relation to its volume, be inert and be easy to rinse.

Bioballs® have almost twice as much surface area in relation to volume as volcanic lapillus, and both have a higher ratio to plastic bottle caps. It is important to fill the biofilter container as much as possible, but even so the surface area provided by the media may not be sufficient to ensure adequate biofiltration, so it is a good idea to oversize the biofilter during initial construction, but knowing that secondary biofilters can be added later if necessary. Biofilters need to be shaken from time to time to avoid clogging, as well as rinsed to avoid being clogged by solid waste that can create an anoxic zone.

Another 'ingredient' required for biofilter is aeration. Nitrifying bacteria need adequate access to oxygen to oxidise ammonia. A simple solution is to use an air pump, placing porous stones connected to an air inlet at the bottom of the container. This ensures that the bacteria have a constantly high concentration of dissolved oxygen. Air pumps can also help to break down any solid or suspended waste not captured by the mechanical separator by shaking and continuously moving the floating Bioballs®. To trap additional solids inside the biofilter, it is also possible to insert a small cylindrical plastic bucket with a nylon mesh, or sponges at the biofilter inlet.

The waste is trapped by this secondary mechanical filter, allowing water to flow over through small holes drilled in the bottom of the bucket into the biofilter container.

Mineralization

Mineralization, from the point of view of aquaponics, refers to the way solid waste is treated and metabolized by bacteria into plant nutrients. Solid waste that is trapped by the mechanical filter contains nutrients; although the processing of this waste is different from biofiltration which requires separate treatment. Keeping solids within the overall system increases the nutrients available to plants. Waste that remains in mechanical filters, biofilters or growth beds undergoes certain mineralization processes. Leaving the waste in place for longer allows for more mineralization. However, this same solid waste component, if not properly managed and mineralized, will block the water flow, consuming oxygen and leading to anoxic conditions, which in turn will produce dangerous hydrogen sulphide gas. Some large systems therefore deliberately leave the solid waste inside the filters, ensuring an adequate flow of water and oxygenation, so that maximum nutrients are released. However, this method is impractical for craft NFT and DWC systems.

If you decide to deliberately "mineralize" these solids, there are simple ways to assist the bacteria in the action in a separate container, simply by adequate oxygenation through air diffused by porous stones. After some time, the solid waste will be consumed, metabolized and transformed by heterotrophic bacteria. At this point, the water can flow back into the aquaponic system and the residual waste, which will be reduced in volume, can be added to the soil.

Alternatively, these solid wastes can be immediately separated, removed and added to any agricultural soil, garden or compost as a valuable

fertilizer. However, immediately extracting these nutrients from the system can be the cause of deficiencies in plants that may require nutrient supplementation.

A compromise solution may be to use a grow bed (e.g. expanded clay or lapillus) for a combination of mechanical and biological filtration.

It is also possible to use a combination of a grow bed for mechanical and biofiltration followed by an NFT system and/or DWC unit.

This can be important where there is no possibility to have the necessary materials to make a turbulence separator and/or a separate biofilter. suffice it to say that for every 200 g of fish feed per day the biofilter must have a volume of 300 litres. The small gravel filter can provide adequate biofiltration for about 20 kg of fish. Although this grow bed would be adequate to provide adequate biofiltration for an NFT or DWC unit as well as capture and retain solid waste, an additional solid waste capture device inserted in the bed is sometimes recommended to prevent the grow bed from clogging itself with solids produced by fish in the long run. Ultimately, since the beds should also be rinsed periodically to remove the solid waste, it is in any case better to provide easy to maintain mechanical filtration upstream of the grow beds.

Summing up

A certain level of filtration is essential for all aquaponic systems the amount of fish stored; the type of system determines the amount of filtration needed. Mechanical filters separate solid waste to avoid toxic accumulations and convert dissolved nitrogenous waste into nitrate through biofiltration.

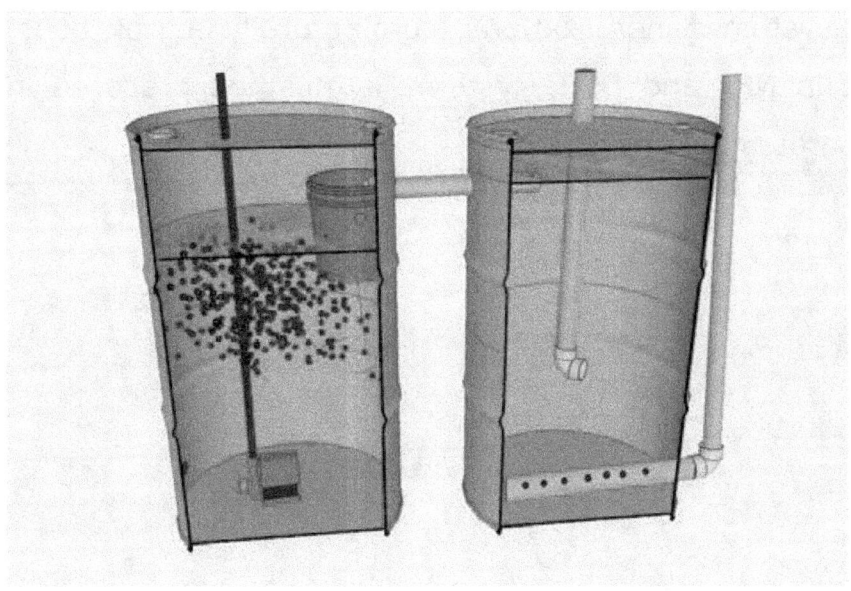

The grow beds themselves act both as mechanical filters and biofilters when using this technique, but additional mechanical filtration is sometimes necessary for high fish densities (15 kg / m3).

Without the grow beds, such as in NFT and DWC units, filtration is always necessary.

Mineralization of solid waste returns more nutrients to the system. Mineralization occurs naturally in grow beds, but in NFT and DWC systems it must be prepared in separate containers.

CHAPTER 4 - Media Beds, NFT, DWC

Hydroponic component is the term to describe the section of the plant where the planets grow. There are several drawings, three of which are discussed in detail in this article. These three models are: medium bed unit, where plants grow in a substrate; nutrient film technique (NFT), where plants grow with their roots in large tubes with a water culture thread; and deep water culture (DWC), also called water raft or floating systems, where plants are suspended above a water reservoir using a floating raft. Each method has advantages and disadvantages. See Sections 4.3-4.6 for details of each.

Water movement is essential to keep all organisms alive in the aquaponics. The flow of water flows from the fish tanks, through the mechanical separator and biofilter and finally reaches the plants in their media beds, pipes or channels, which collect the dissolved nutrients.

If the water movement stops, the most immediate effect will be an OD reduction and the accumulation of waste in the fish tank.

A common guideline for densely populated aquaponic systems is to have two water changes per hour. For example, if an aquaponic unit has a total water volume of 1000 litres, the water flow rate should be 2000 litres/hr, so that every hour the water is renewed twice. However, in case of low storage density the water only needs to be recycled once every hour. There are three commonly used methods to keep water moving through a system: submersible impeller pumps, airlifts and human energy.

Water movement

The movement of water is essential to keep all organisms alive in the aquaponics. The flow of water flows from the fish tanks, through the mechanical separator and biofilter and finally reaches the plants in their media beds, pipes or channels, which collect the dissolved nutrients.

If the water movement stops, the most immediate effect will be an OD reduction and the accumulation of waste in the fish tank.

A common guideline for densely populated aquaponic systems is to have two water changes per hour. For example, if an aquaponic unit has a total water volume of 1000 litres, the water flow rate should be 2000 litres/hr, so that every hour the water is renewed twice. However, in case of low storage density the water only needs to be recycled once every hour. There are three commonly used methods to keep water moving through a system: submersible impeller pumps, airlifts and human energy.

Submersible water pump

The heart of an aquaponic system is almost always a submersible impeller pump, this type of pump is recommended.

In order to ensure a long service life and energy efficiency, high quality water pumps should preferably be used. High quality pumps can maintain their pumping capacity and efficiency for a period of 3-5 years, while lower quality products will lose pumping power in a shorter time and significantly reduce water flows. As far as flow rate is concerned, the small units described in this work need a flow rate of 2000 litre/h for a maximum height of 1.5 metres; a submersible pump of this capacity would have consumed 25-50 W/h.

A useful approximation to calculate the energy required for submersible pumps is that a pump can move 40 litres of water per hour for every watt per hour consumed, although some models are twice as efficient.

When designing the hydraulic sizing of the pump, it is important to realize that during pumping there is a loss of energy at each connection; up to 5 percent of the total flow rate can be lost at each pipe connection when water is forced through it. Therefore, use the minimum number of connections possible. It is also important to note that the smaller the pipe diameter, the greater the loss of water flow. A 30mm pipe has twice the flow rate of a 20mm pipe, even if served by pumps of the same capacity.

In addition, a larger pipe requires no maintenance to remove the accumulation of solids inside it. In practical terms, this translates into significant savings in electricity and operating costs. When installing an aquaponic system, be sure to place the submersible pump in an accessible location for periodic cleaning. In fact, the internal filter will need cleaning every 2-3 weeks. Submersible water pumps will break if they are operated without water.

Airlifts

Airlifts are another water lifting technique that uses an air pump rather than a water pump.

The air is forced to the bottom of a pipe inside the fish tank, the rising of the bubbles towards the surface allows the water to be carried along with them. One of the advantages is that airlifts are more energy efficient, but they can only lift water up to limited heights (30-40 cm). One advantage of airlifts is that they oxygenate the water during its transport through air bubbles.

Finally, air pumps generally have a longer life than submerged water pumps. Finally, there is the advantage that only one airlift pump can be purchased for both aeration and water circulation, which reduces the expense for a second pump.

Muscular strength

Some aquaponic systems are designed to use human force to move water.

Water can be lifted in buckets or using pulleys, modified bicycles or other means. An expansion vessel can be filled manually and placed to drain slowly throughout the day. These methods are only applicable for small systems and should only be considered if electricity is not available or is not reliable. Often these systems will have low OD and insufficient mixing of nutrients.

Ventilation

Air pumps inject air into the water through pipes and porous stones inside fish tanks, thus increasing OD levels in the water.

Additional dissolved oxygen is an essential component of NFT and DWC units. The air is diffused through small porous stones.

The smaller the bubbles, the better the oxygen will be distributed. Small bubbles have more surface area and therefore release water oxygen better than large bubbles; this makes the aeration system more efficient and contributes to cost containment. It is therefore recommended to use quality air stones in order to obtain small air bubbles. Air stones should be cleaned regularly first with a chlorine solution to kill bacterial deposits and then, if necessary, with a slightly acidic substance to remove mineralization or they should be replaced when the bubble flow is insufficient. The quality of air pumps is an irreplaceable component of aquaponic systems, many systems have been saved from catastrophic collapse by an abundance of OD.

For small units, consisting of a 1000 litre tank, it is recommended that at least two air lines with stones, also called injectors, are placed in the fish tank as well as an injector in the biofilter container.

Venturi Siphons

Low-tech and easy to build Venturi siphons are another technique to increase OD levels in aquaponic systems. This technique is particularly useful in DWC channels.

To put it simply, Venturi siphons use a hydrodynamic principle to "suck" air from outside (suction) when pressurized water flows at a higher speed through a smaller diameter pipe section. With constant water flow, if the diameter of the hose decreases, the water velocity must increase, and this higher velocity creates a negative pressure. Venturi siphons are short sections of pipe (20 mm diameter, 5 cm long) inserted into the main pipe of larger diameter (25 mm). Since the water in the main pipe is forced through the narrow section, it creates a jet effect.

Media bed technique

Growbeds filled with an inert medium is the most widely used system in small-scale aquaponic systems. This system is strongly recommended in most developing regions because it allows efficient use of space, has a relatively low initial cost and is suitable for beginners because of its simplicity. In growbeds filled with a medium, the inert material is used to support plant roots but also acts as a filter, both mechanical and biological. This dual function is the main reason why such systems are simpler. In the following paragraphs we explain why NFT and DWC methods require specific and more complicated components for filtration. However, the inert filled growbed technique is cumbersome and relatively expensive for large-scale systems. The medium's bed may become clogged if fish stocking densities exceed the loading capacity of the beds and this may require separate filtration. Water evaporation is higher in inert filled beds due to the larger surface area exposed to the sun. Finally, some media are very heavy.

There are many designs for growth beds that use different media, also for this reason it is the technique that is more adaptable to different situations.

Water flow dynamics

The figure shows the main components of an aquaponic system with beds filled with inert material. You can see the fish tank, the growth beds, the pumping sump, as well as the concrete blocks for the support. Reading the drawing is easier to understand, following the flow of water through the system. The water flows by gravity from the fish tank, the beds are filled with porous inert material which also acts as a biofilter.

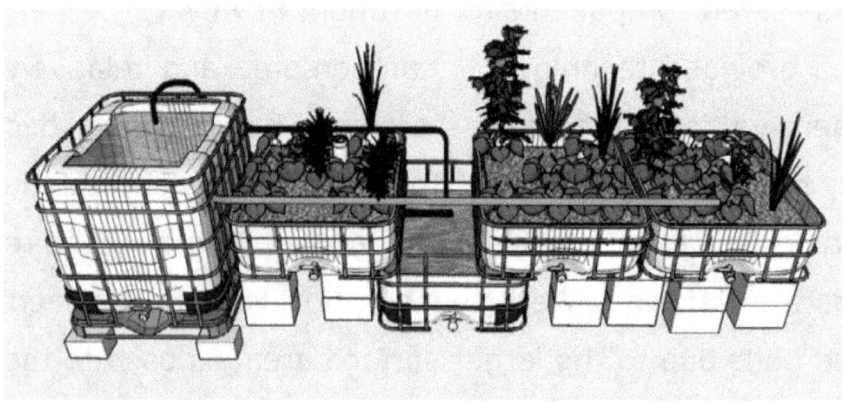

The beds house the colony of nitrifying bacteria and provide a suitable place for plant growth. At the exit of the growbeds, the water continues to the cockpit tank, still by gravity. At this point, the water is relatively free of solid waste in solution and is pumped to the fish reservoir, from where it starts again to the growth beds, resuming the cycle. Some growth beds are designed to get completely wet and then drain, which means that the water level rises at a certain point and then drains completely.

This adds oxygen to the roots of the plants and helps in the biofiltration of ammonia. Other irrigation methods use a constant flow of water, either by feeding it from one side of the bed and leaving the other, or by distributing it through a drip irrigation system.

Construction of a Growbed

We describe how to build an aquaponic plant that is based on the cultivation technology called grow bed.

This is because such a system can be considered among the cheapest, as well as the most suitable for those who are new to aquaponics. However, there are also other cultivation methods used in both aquaponics and hydroponics, using, for example, vertical towers, NFT, and DWC (deep water crops).

The peculiarity of the grow bed system is that the element intended to house the plants, the "growth bed", also acts as a mechanical and biological filter.

Therefore, the elements that constitute an aquaponic system with a growth bed are:

- fish tank
- bed of growth
- sump tub.

To build such a system, first you must make a hole on one of the sides of the fish tank, at a height that will be used to regulate the water level inside the tank. In fact, by means of a pipe that will fish in the lowest part, the water will come out to pour into the "growth bed" positioned on the side, at a slightly lower level.

The "growth bed" must be equipped with a bell-shaped siphon that will allow the continuous filling and emptying of the grow bed.

The growth bed is made up of a container containing inert material which, as already mentioned, guarantees a certain mechanical filtration and allows plant roots and bacteria to anchor and develop. Among the most used and common inert materials, given the low cost and easy availability, there is expanded clay: this substrate, together with the mechanism of the bell siphon, facilitates the oxygenation of plant roots and keeps them anchored.

The water that comes out of the bed through the siphon will be conveyed to the collection tank in which we will place the pump that will bring it back to the fish tank, starting the cycle again.

Once we understand how it works, the possible configurations and experiments are endless, and this is the beauty of it.

Philip L. Malave
Aquaponics for Beginners

CHAPTER 5 - Aquaponics how to make a plant

Aquaponics makes the water filter and plant fertilizer useless, transforming the plant into a self-sufficient mini ecosystem in which waste is recycled from the roots, which filters the water at the same time.

Although no soil and fish farming techniques are very old, the combination of the two is recent and can be traced back to the early 1970s.

Studied all over the world, it is particularly interesting for the reduction of space and costs, for the very low production of organic waste. An ideal activity in schools, it offers educational cues allowing to clarify the concept of biological circle and synergy between living organisms.

The natural union that binds plants, fish and water is evident and obvious, and it is surprising that the relationship was exploited and deepened relatively late.

Fish need a clean, well-oxygenated environment and adequate nutrition.

They produce solid and liquid waste, which if left to accumulate without proper filtration will irreparably pollute the environment and kill the guests.

In our system, the organic waste in question is attacked by nitrifying bacteria.

Plants absorb ammonium and nitrate during the assimilation process, after which they are converted into organic molecules containing nitrogen.

When the nitrogen-based nutrients have fulfilled their function, specialised decomposing bacteria begin a process known as denitrification.

Put simply, during the process plants can absorb the elements they need, while eliminating pollution and providing a healthy environment for fish.

In the Virgin Islands a team of researchers has developed a project to import this technique especially in the archipelagos where most agricultural products must be imported, and the catch is declining.

The University of Davis in California is working on the adaptation of the concept of "family farm". (family farm) providing for the use of aquaponics in the domestic environment for recreational, educational, decorative purposes and to produce biologically on a small to medium scale.

What does it take to start?

- A fish tank and a support for plants
- Bacteria for decomposing fish waste
- A filter to host bacteria and ventilate the tank
- Fish and fish food
- Plants
- pH regulators and tests, micro and macro-element supplements, to make up for any nutritional deficiencies.
- Equipment for plants and fish

You can obtain the tank, the bacteria and the filter to house them from a pet or aquarium product shop. Bacteria do indeed develop naturally within this mini-ecosystem in about 3 weeks, but in order not to take any risks and not to let them run wild for so long it is worth investing in their purchase, also considering that their number can vary and it could be useful to have more of them within reach.

As far as the hydroponic system is concerned, it is possible to choose the type that suits us best: NFT for slower and "soft" growth or aero-hydroponic for dynamic and explosive results, for example.

Oxygenation in this context assumes an essential importance for the correct development of the hosts.

The other determining factors for a good success do not differ much from the traditional ones that are respected in the grow rooms: adequate temperature, cleanliness, good ventilation.

The hydroponic system should simply be positioned above the aquarium and equipped with a pump to create water recirculation.

Fishes

There are several suitable species to choose from.

It is essential that they are cold water fish and not tropical, as they do not like brackish or salt water.

You can buy them all the same or different species; only make sure at the time of purchase that they are compatible breeds and suitable for the size and temperature.

In the greenhouses we have chosen koi carp, a very strong fish of Japanese origin, which can withstand environmental variations well. They are beautiful, colourful, inexpensive animals; although they reach considerable size in the wild, they do not grow much when kept in aquariums.

Plants

You can choose virtually any type of plant.

If it is a commercial plant, a species that thrives in nitrogen-rich environments, such as lettuce or herbs, is preferable.

In fact, it is the food fed to the fish that determines the type of fertilisation of the plants, and there are none commercially available with different amounts of NPK to choose from.

However, if you are an amateur grower, you can venture into the choice of plants according to your personal taste: decorative, edible, medicinal, aromatic and so on.

The important thing is to maintain a balanced ratio between the number of fish and the number of plants to ensure a healthy environment, avoiding toxicity and deficiencies.

Fish nutrition is an important element: it must be of good quality and it is important to make sure that the fish consume it all and do not remain leftovers to decompose in the aquarium.

The best food is live fish. Most fish feed on other fish: it is a very rich and healthy food that forces aquarium guests to chase and catch their prey, an exercise that keeps them healthy and reproduces the natural lifestyle.

It is also possible to produce a balanced food at home following the retailer's instructions; for those who want a 100% organic harvest this is certainly the best choice.

Whatever diet your fish follow, there may be a nutritional deficiency. Quite common is the iron deficiency, which can be made up for by adding a few drops of Bio Essentials (a mix of micro and macro-elements that provides a mixture of iron chelates) every 2 or 3 weeks.

How to start?

First, the aquarium:

- For the well-being of the fish, it is good to put clean aquarium gravel on the bottom.
- Fill the tank slowly with tap water, taking care to put a plastic sheet on the sand in the bottom and a bowl on the plastic: this way the gravel will remain in place.
- Activate the filter and let it turn 24 hours to give time for the chlorine to evaporate (if you don't want to wait buy the special

product in the shop where you bought the fish).

- Important: before introducing the guests, stabilize the pH level at 7, mediating between the acidic environment of 6.5 required by the plants and the slightly basic environment preferred by the fish (7.5).

This operation requires the use of the pH tester and good brand regulators, we use the GHE pH Down powder formula.

It is worth noting that in hydroponics water is usually acidic (5 - 6.5), because it is with these values that plants best assimilate mineral salts. With higher values there is a lowering of the radical absorption capacity, which is why it is recommended to supplement with special products.

- Add the bacteria: two-thirds in the filter, one-third directly on the gravel.

- Add the fish, being careful to choose young specimens that can adapt to the best.

If you have taken them home as you usually do in plastic bags, it is a good idea to leave them about half an hour in their soaking bags in the aquarium, so that they can gradually adapt to the new temperature and have less shock.

- You can now place the plant holders on the tank and fix them securely.
- Now wait 2 - 3 days for the fish to start producing waste and the bacteria to turn it into fertiliser, then introduce the plants.

Philip L. Malave
Aquaponics for Beginners

CHAPTER 6 - How to Make an Aquaponic System at Home

Prepare the Frame

You need the Antonius frame for the main structure. It will consist of one or two baskets and two plastic containers. Use the 50 litres container as a fish tank at the bottom and the 25-litre container for the growth bed at the top. Assemble all parts, based on the relevant package instructions.

Use the basket as a support for the 25-litre plastic container that will house the growth bed. It is not strictly necessary to have the 50-litre plastic container for the fish tank at the base if you just put it on the floor. You should cut the plastic edge of the top container to ensure a better fit; in this tutorial, the handles have also been cut from the end of the container. However, this is not strictly necessary. To cut the plastic, use a small saw or standard wire stripper pliers.

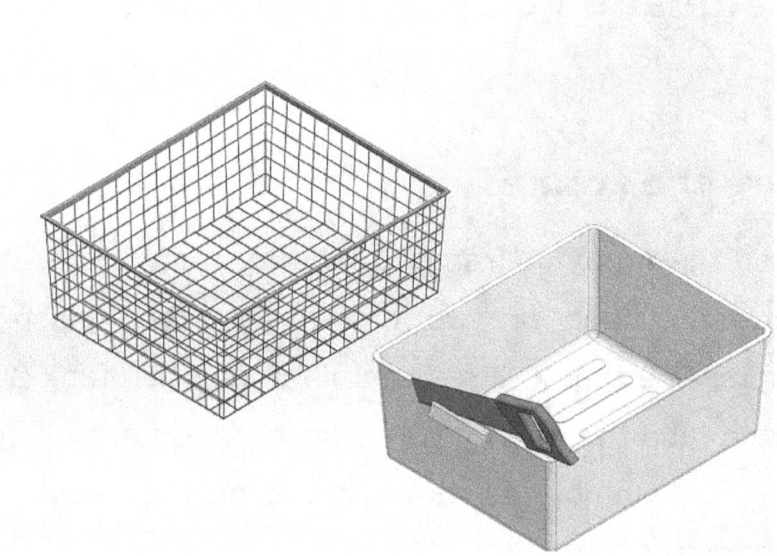

If you want to customize the system to suit the style of your decor, now is the time to do so. The pictures show an example of a fish tank that has been decorated with a strip of PVC.

Hydraulic System

The plumbing for the aquaponic system is not too complicated and you can rely on a few basic principles to help make the system as efficient as possible.

Use a small 600 litres/hour submersible electric pump in a corner of the fish tank that will carry the water to the growth bed. The water flows through the growth bed and out in the opposite corner to the inlet. When the water returns to the fish tank, it pushes any solid waste back to the pump, which will carry it to the growth bed.

Use a by-pass valve in this system. This diverts some of the water from the pump back into the fish tank. This allows you to control the amount of water that will serve the growth bed, while the diverted water creates movement in the fish tank, as well as providing additional ventilation. In this tutorial, 13mm PVC pipes have been used for the entire system. Initially, you should also start with the growth bed and siphon used here.

Get the male and female threaded adapters. Drill a hole in the right place in the growth bed - you need to make sure the female adapter fits into the square of the frame grid. Make the hole about 6 or 7 centimetres from the edge of the housing in each direction; the hole should fit perfectly with the male threaded adapter.

Thread the male adapter through the top of the growth bed. Then mount rubber gaskets on the threads. Then screw the female adapter to the male adapter until a complete, watertight fit is achieved. If you want, but it is not strictly necessary, you can add silicone on the bottom. Finally, use a reducer on top of the male adapter. The one shown here is a reducer from 25mm to 13mm.

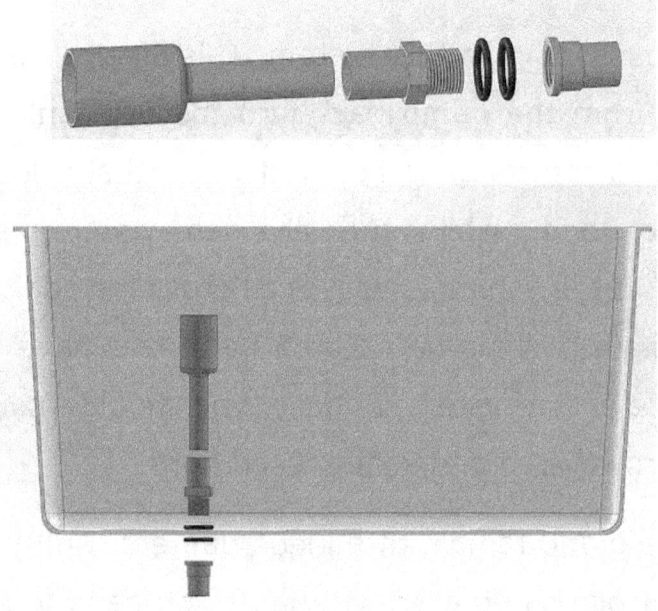

This whole piece is called a standpipe and will allow water to flow out of the growth bed. It is advisable that the overall height is about 2.5 cm below the top of the growth bed; therefore, you will need to cut the tube so that it is at the right height. At this point, let the silicone dry if you have used any.

The Siphon

The bell siphon is a very effective method of slowly flooding the growth bed and then quickly draining the water. And it does this with a non-mechanical action, moreover, it has no moving parts that can break.

Place the 60mm bell siphon in the middle. This is a 60mm piece of pipe with an airtight cap on top. The bell-shaped siphon is shown in the photos with some cut pieces on the bottom, with some holes on the sides - it is advisable that these holes are not higher than about 2.5 cm from the bottom of the tube. The water will drain down to this level and then stop.

Finally, the 100mm protection simply keeps the growth bed material away from the bell siphon. The protection has holes drilled or cut out to allow water to enter - and keep the roots and material out! The cap is optional, but it helps keep things out of the bell siphon.

Bell siphons can be complicated to operate. The mechanics of a siphon trap are relatively complex, but you just need to worry about the practical application of the siphons, so you can quickly empty a growth bed into a tank or fish tank using a simple mechanical method with no electrical or moving parts.

Bypass ball valve

Add a bypass ball valve. This allows you to control how much water flows into the growth bed and is therefore an important addition. The bypass ball valve also allows you to divert water to the fish tank, providing additional aeration and water movement in the tank. This improves fish health.

Philip L. Malave
Aquaponics for Beginners

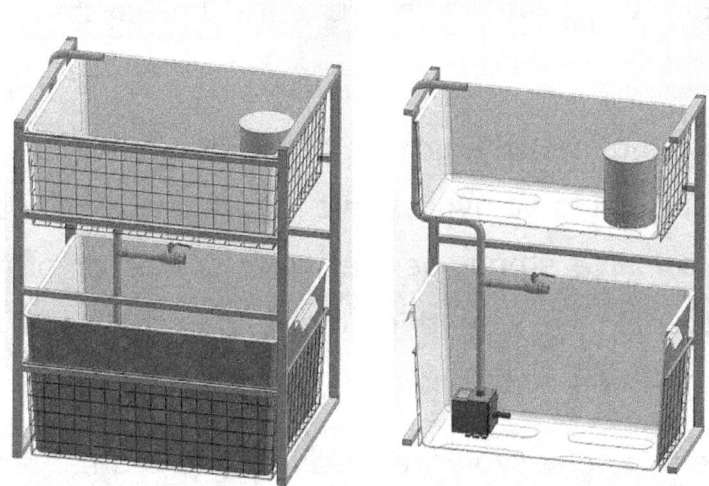

In the pictures shown you can see the small 600 litres/hour pump with a small piece of 13 mm tube inserted. This then has a T-piece attached and continues up to the 90-degree elbow at the top, which brings the water to the growth bed with a 13 mm tube. In the second outlet of the T-piece there is a simple ball valve that controls the flow of water that is diverted back into the fish tank.

Once you have assembled the whole assembly with the frame, containers and plumbing, add water to the fish tank and start the pump. Test to see if everything is working properly and to make sure the system is watertight!

Fill the top container (the growth bed) with some growth material. This could be hydro tonic (aggregate expanded clay pellets), lava stone, perlite, river stones or other similar material. Use something that allows the water to flow through the growth bed and that is not toxic.

Once all this is done, you are ready to add the fish and start putting the plants into the system. Initially, just add a couple of small fish, just to start producing the ammonia needed to start the system.

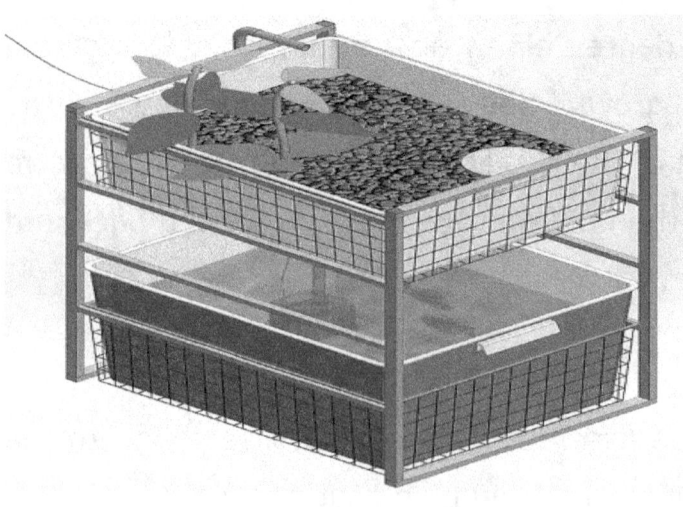

Warnings

Make sure that all pipes are tightly tightened together to prevent leakage. The systems shown in this tutorial are not glued together because a constant push is usually enough!

Philip L. Malave
Aquaponics for Beginners

CHAPTER 7 - Which plants?

To date, more than 150 different vegetables, herbs, flowers and small trees have successfully grown in aquaponic systems, including research, domestic and commercial units. In general, green leafy plants perform very well in aquaponics along with some of the most popular fruit vegetables, including tomatoes, cucumbers and peppers. Fruit and vegetables require more nutrients and are more appropriate in established systems with adequate quantities of fish. However, some tubers and sensitive plants do not grow well in aquaponics. Tubers require special attention, and grow successfully only in medium depth beds, or in a version of breathable beds.

Vegetables vary in relation to their overall nutrient demand. There are two general categories of aquaponic plants based on this demand. Low nutrient demand plants include green leafy vegetables and herbs such as lettuce, thistle, rocket, basil, mint, parsley, coriander, chives, bock choi and watercress. Many legumes such as peas and beans also have a low level of nutrient demand. On the other side of the spectrum are plants with high nutrient demand, sometimes called nutrient hungry.

These include fruits such as tomatoes, eggplants, cucumbers, zucchini, strawberries and peppers. Other plants with medium nutrient demand are cabbage, such as cabbage, cauliflower, broccoli and kohlrabi. Bulbous plants such as beets, taro, onions and carrots have an average demand, while radishes require less nutrients.

The growth bed style influences the choice of plants. In medium-bed units, it is common practice to grow polyculture such as green leaves, herbs and fruits at the same time.

By providing medium growth beds at the right depth (at least 30 cm) it is possible to grow all the vegetables mentioned above. Polyculture on small areas can also benefit from complementary plants and better space management, because shade-loving species can grow under taller plants. Mono-crop practices are prevalent in NFT and DWC units because the grower is limited by the number of holes in the pipes and the floats in which to plant the vegetables. Using NFT units, it may be possible to grow vegetables with larger fruits, such as tomatoes, but these plants need plenty of water to ensure an enough supply of nutrients and avoid water stress. Withering in fruit plants can occur almost immediately if the flow is interrupted, with devastating effects on the entire crop. Fruit plants also need to be planted in larger tubes, ideally with flat bottoms, and placed at a greater distance from vegetables and green leaves. This is because fruit plants grow bigger and need more light to ripen and because there is limited space for the roots in the tubes. On the other hand, large bulbs and/or tubers, such as kohlrabi, carrots and turnips, are more likely to be grown in medium beds because NFT and DWC units do not provide a good growing environment and adequate support for the plants. It is important to consider the effects of plant harvesting on the whole ecosystem. If all the plants were collected at once, the result would be an unbalanced system without enough plants to clean the water, resulting in nutrient peaks.

Some farmers use this technique, but it must correspond with a large collection of fish or a reduction in feed intake. However, the recommendation is to use staggered harvesting and a reseeding cycle. The presence of too many plants growing at the same time could result in a system with nutrient deficiency towards the harvest period, when uptake is at its maximum. Having plants at different stages of growth, for example some seedlings and some mature plants, the overall demand for nutrients is always the same. This ensures more stable water chemistry and offers more regular production for both the domestic table and the market.

CHAPTER 8 - Which Fishes in Aquaponics?

If you do not know which fish to use in aquaponics, know that you have many possibilities: from red shrimp to tilapia, from trout to freshwater mussel, up to gilthead sea bream (Sparus aurata) and sea bass (Dicentrarchus labrax), also known as sea bass, two fish for which the possibility of breeding in fresh water has been demonstrated, with lower growth rates than salt water, but managing to maintain the organoleptic characteristics unchanged.

Let's see together in more detail which aquaponic fish to choose and their possible combinations to obtain a multi-trophic plant, depending on whether we are interested in production or just for ornamental purposes.

First of all, it is useful to know that for ornamental species, especially koi, the volume of water available must be taken into account: to keep the fish healthy and ensure adequate growth and good colour development, a high volume is required (at least 1000 litres per koi and

100-150 for goldfish). If we must build a production plant, high fish densities of up to 20 kg/m3 will be required.

We recommend the use of ornamental species for aquaponic systems intended for decorative use or for small domestic production plants (up to 5 thousand litres) as they need a lower mass and density of fish than commercial production plants and this allows to create less stressful conditions for our fish which for this reason will develop their colours in the best way.

Among the ornamental species in aquaculture it is possible to breed koi carp, together with goldfish, sturgeon, gambusia and gobion, as they live together in nature without bothering each other.

Carp koi, gambusie and medaka

We advise you to pay attention to the gambusia, as they are an alien species introduced in the past to fight mosquitoes, but they are very voracious also towards smaller fish, as well as towards eggs and tadpoles, so they can represent a danger if dispersed in the environment.

A very valid alternative to the mosquito is represented by the medaka, also called rice fish or mini-carps koi, which have a much more docile character towards the other species. They originate from Japan, imported into Italy only recently and are similar in size and appearance to gambusia. Moreover, the medaka are very lively fish and do not fear the presence of man, swimming on the surface of the water and giving, thanks to their bright colouring (hence the name of mini koi), a remarkable aesthetic performance and pleasant moments of relaxation.

Feeding: In nature, carp are omnivorous and feed on a wide range of foods, they prefer feeding invertebrates such as: aquatic insects, larvae, worms, molluscs and zooplankton. Some species of grass carp also eat the stems, leaves and seeds of aquatic and terrestrial plants, as well as rotting vegetation.

Reproduction: The best carp fry is obtained from dedicated hatcheries and breeding facilities. The procedure for obtaining fry is more complicated than that used for tilapia, because spawning in female carp is induced by an injection of hormones, a technique that requires a good knowledge of fish physiology and experience.

Gobion, sturgeon and shellfish

As far as the gobion is concerned, it is a very quiet bottom fish compared to other species and needs very low levels of nitrites.

Also, the sturgeon is indicated in an ornamental plant, as it is a fish capable of reaching remarkable dimensions, standing out among the others and becoming in a short time the undisputed protagonist of our body of water.

As far as molluscs are concerned, Planorbarius and Physa marmorata are very suitable, two types of gastropod molluscs that perform an important action, avoiding the accumulation of unconsumed feed, maintaining a cleaner environment and at the same time guaranteeing the complete conversion of the feed not consumed by the fish, so as to optimize the fertilization of the plants. These molluscs also have a further function, they are in fact bio-indicators for the lack of calcium and magnesium carbonates dissolved in water, through the appearance of white lines and deformations of the shell that increase over time.

Fish in Aquaponics for food purposes

Among the most suitable species are Tilapia, redclaw lobster, perch, sun perch, yellow perch, catfish, trout perch and other types of shrimps and molluscs, such as the Anodonta cygnea.

Tilapia

It is one of the most consumed species in the world, in Asia, and lends itself very well to be bred in tanks. In recent years this fish has gained a bad reputation because of the techniques with which it is bred in order to lower costs, i.e. using animal waste instead of feed for the juvenile stage, with the result that its meat is up to 10 times more polluted than wild specimens. We "aquaponists" are convinced that by using a healthy and balanced diet, accompanied by better water quality due to the phyto-purification of plants, the quality and healthiness of this fish can improve considerably compared to the standard on the market.

Nutrition: Tilapies are omnivorous, which means that they have a diet that includes both substances of animal and vegetable origin. They also eat other fish, especially their young; when they are in farming conditions they must be kept separate according to size. While specimens smaller than 15 cm eat smaller fish, when they are larger than 15 cm, they are generally too slow and cease to be a problem for smaller fish.

Reproduction: Tilapias reproduce easily, especially where the water is warm, oxygenated, there is algae, the basin is shaded and the environment calm and peaceful. A rocky substratum on the bottom encourages the construction of the nest. The optimal ratio between males and females is 2 males for every 6-10 females. The fry should be transferred into breeding tanks until the juvenile stages, ensuring that there is no larger fry that could eat them.

Red crayfish (redclaw lobster)

It is a crayfish, particularly suitable in aquaponics in DWC (Deep Water Culture) systems, as its presence helps to keep the roots clean of accumulated organic matter, insects or other small animals. This type of crayfish is successfully grown together with tilapia.

Real perch

It is a fish that lives in both fresh and brackish water, very valuable in the kitchen for its meat and is present in many Italian lakes such as Como and Trasimeno. The perch can reach 60 cm in length and 30 years of age, it is a diurnal and carnivorous fish.

In addition to the royal perch you can also use the trout perch, sun perch and bass "striped bass".

Diet: The trout perch is a carnivorous fish and requires diets rich in protein. They must all be bred the same size to avoid predation of the juveniles by the larger fish.

Aptitude: From a nutritional point of view, trout perch contains relatively high levels of omega-3 fatty acids compared to other freshwater fish.

Anodonta cygnea

Also known as freshwater mussel, it is a bivalve that lives in slow or stagnant watercourses and needs a muddy substrate in which it can establish itself, hiding completely under the sand and thus helping to keep the bottom oxygenated, also avoiding the formation of anoxia zones. The Anodonta cyngea has an enormous filtering capacity that can reach 40 litres per hour, it needs a Ph between 7 and 8, because at lower Ph, the calcium carbonate that makes up its shell begins to melt, quickly leading to the death of the animal: for this reason it is not recommended for the cultivation of strawberries and in general of all those plants that give their best to acid Ph.

This animal feeds on organic matter suspended in the water, but also on protozoa and other microorganisms, many of which are parasites or cause diseases for our fish, accumulating them as a reservoir inside its body. This characteristic represents on the one hand an advantage as it helps to keep the aquatic environment clean and healthy, but at the same time it is good to always keep an eye on freshwater mussels as if they die, in a short time they release all the filtered pollutants, causing significant damage, such as the appearance of diseases or worsening water conditions.

Trout

It is a freshwater fish that lives in streams and mountain lakes, with cold (below 25 degrees) and oxygenated water. There are various types, ranging from rainbow trout, salmon trout, marmorata, up to rainbow trout, the most widespread and resistant even to less oxygenated waters and warmer temperatures.

This last one, compared to the other varieties, is more suitable for the aquaponic cultivation, and considering the commercial value of this fish, we shall soon see many productive plants which will use it.

Nutrition: Trout require a diet richer in proteins than carp and Tilapia, being a carnivorous and not omnivorous species, which means a greater quantity of nitrogen available in the water in relation to the nutrients introduced in the tank.

Suitability: Trout are considered a "fatty fish", with a high amount of vitamin A, vitamin D and omega-3 fatty acids, making them an excellent choice for family consumption.

Sea bass

Also known by the name of sea bass, it is a seawater fish found in all seas, very delicious for its meat. It is a light and digestible fish, with just 97 kcal, 18 grams of protein and 1.7 grams of fat per 100 grams.

It has recently been demonstrated that it can also be reared in brackish and fresh water, managing to maintain its organoleptic characteristics unchanged, but with a drop in growth rates.

It certainly represents a valid choice to make the aquaponic production as sustainable as possible.

Sea bream

It is the seawater fish famous for the golden spot between the eyes and very famous for its lean and tasty meat.

It has a high content of essential amino acids, as well as mostly polyunsaturated and monounsaturated fats. The cholesterol intake is very low, just 65 mg per 100 grams, therefore perfect for low-calorie diets, but also for those suffering from diabetes and obesity.

Recently it has been possible to adapt sea bream to fresh water, thus allowing its use in aquaponics.

Having made some first important distinctions, we will continue in the future to provide you with further advice on which fish you prefer for aquaponics: we too are always looking for new ornamental species and not that can be bred, even in combination.

CONCLUSION

Thank you for making it through to the end of this book, let's hope it was informative and able to provide you with all the tools you need to achieve your goals whatever they may be.

Aquaponics has emerged as a great way to lose growing genuine and tasty vegetable products at home for good health. Yet, many people fail to get all the benefits of this wonderful process due to lack of knowledge of the process. This book has tried to bring all the important points to the fore so that you can get all the benefits of aquaponic without having to deal with the negative effects.

All you must do is follow the information provided in the book and follow the directions.

You can also get all the benefits of the process by following the simple steps in the book.

I hope that this book will really help you achieve your goals.

Philip L. Malave
Aquaponics for Beginners

Philip L. Malave
Aquaponics for Beginners

Philip L. Malave
Aquaponics for Beginners

www.ingramcontent.com/pod-product-compliance
Lightning Source LLC
Chambersburg PA
CBHW070929080526
44589CB00013B/1444